MIMEOGRAPH

poems by

David Colodney

Finishing Line Press
Georgetown, Kentucky

MIMEOGRAPH

Copyright © 2019 by David Colodney
ISBN 978-1-64662-101-9 First Edition
All rights reserved under International and Pan-American Copyright Conventions. No part of this book may be reproduced in any manner whatsoever without written permission from the publisher, except in the case of brief quotations embodied in critical articles and reviews.

ACKNOWLEDGMENTS

Several of these poems have appeared in various journals. My heartfelt thanks to the editors who chose them and the readers who read them:

"Biscayne Bay Lies Still, Like Glass" appeared in *Panoply* and was an editor's choice selection
"615 84th Street, Apt. 4" appeared in *The Chaffin Review*
"At George's Wake" and "Five Years" were featured in *Night Owl*
"Stuck Between Stations," "Matzo Brei in Four Easy Steps, and "615 84th Street" were published by *Gyroscope Review*
"Twilight," and "Sunday Morning Poem" appeared in *Shot Glass Journal*
"One Day I Woke up and There was No One to Take to Basketball Practice" was printed in *California Quarterly*
"Morning Rush" and "Shuttering" appeared in *Cathexis Northwest Press*

Publisher: Leah Maines
Editor: Christen Kincaid
Cover Art: Harriet Colodney
Author Photo: Marta Colodney
Cover Design: Elizabeth Maines McCleavy

Printed in the USA on acid-free paper.
Order online: www.finishinglinepress.com
also available on amazon.com

Author inquiries and mail orders:
Finishing Line Press
P. O. Box 1626
Georgetown, Kentucky 40324
U. S. A.

Table of Contents

Morning Rush 1

Shuttering 2

Biscayne Bay Lies Still Like Glass 3

615 84th Street, Apt. 4 4

10 Things I Think I See in the Blurred TV Screen 5

Matzo Brei in Four Easy Steps 6

At George's Wake 8

My Father's Armchair 9

December 9, 1980 10

Morning in Mourning 11

NYC Story, 1951- 12

Mimeograph 15

Stuck Between Stations 16

Ode to Derek Jeter 17

Incubation 18

Macaroni & Cheese 19

Twilight 20

One Day I Woke up and There Was No One to Take to

    Basketball Practice 21

Five Years 22

Sunday Morning Poem 24

Morning Rush

Morning's rush hour starts before we even leave the house, the paws of the dog leading us down the stairs, the tap, tap tapping of her claws on laminate floors to the kitchen where we calculate the math of the eggs, balancing it with the scramble to get out the door on time. *Do we have enough milk?* We bump against each other in a kitchen tighter than the cellophane that wraps last night's leftovers turned today's lunch, an awkward first dance of the day. *Do we have two slices of bread?* Cutting the moldy edge off in last-minute desperation, the clock tick, tick ticking louder, a doomsday countdown with a metronomic beat. *Dad, Matt's still in the bathroom*, Jakob yells. *Use another one!* I reply *and hurry, hurry, we gotta go!* Adam is away at school and these two are close behind, an assembly line of college visits and college tuition. In quiet times, we worry about affording school while trying to save for retirement, but that can wait. Right now, Jakob doesn't have a clean school shirt, I-95 has two lanes blocked in my direction and we've just run out of coffee.

Shuttering

Mom asks for my dead father ten times a day,
a whisper from an ashen murmur wondering
where he is and when he'll be home from work.
I think of new ways to respond each time.
Mom telephones old friends, people long dead—
like the woman she made me call Aunt Millie
even though we weren't related, conversing
robustly to empty air, perhaps hearing
the rhythms of their answers in the flapping
of our converted guestroom's window drapes.
I politely ask how they are when she hangs up.

Mom leaves food simmering on the stove, forgetting
the broth she boils, or the water for tea, wandering
away into another world hearing other voices until
mine bellows, frustration boiling over like the water
sizzling onto the stovetop as I ask my wife
if we should babyproof the house from her.

Mom can amaze by recalling minute details from 1972—
like organizing the anti-Nixon rally at NYU
or the name of the Filipino student who asked
for her number after—but nothing from the last hour,
memories reduced to an accounting equation:
first in first out, last in, last out
her brain flickering as a failing and loose light bulb
on and off   on and off.

Biscayne Bay Lies Still, Like Glass

My father is buried a few miles north of this place:
where Biscayne Bay oozes against asphalt
and boats drift from marina to bay to sunset.
Latin music and multilingual chit-chat blends,
a symphony in cacophony.

On another anniversary of his death, I walk, beer
in hand sweating droplets back to my elbows.
I've lived most of my life a few miles east of this place.
To the west, people live under bridges.

My father always loved how Miami looks on TV:
pastel glamor, glistening hodge-podge of twinkling
lights. Neon bouncing off the skyline, a relay
from building to building to building,
dusky electricity under glitzy skies.

My beer is nearly drained. I peer south
over a railing and ask the water if I died here,
would I have died happy? The water offers
no advice, doesn't even meander.
In this place: the water lies still like glass.

615 84th Street, Apt. 4

My father sleeping as other fathers worked,
toiling as other fathers slept,
my mother hushing my sisters and me
quiet after school, afternoon glowing
through aluminum foil window blinds

pasted to the windows. My father off to work,
midnight abandoned, my sisters and me asleep,
enveloped in a World War II-era railroad flat. Odd
nights our air conditioner worked, humming
in relentless summer, I dreamed heroic

soldiers once slept in this same room, echoes
standing guard against my apparition father's voice
booming from the kitchen, reflected by a smoldering
cigarette tip in a plastic ashtray,
alive in the smoke rings and past due
bills stacked on the counter

close enough to that ashtray to spark into flames,
if only he had any luck.

10 Things I Think I See Through the Blurred TV Screen

I think I see a minion dressed in black   praying Kaddish
I think I see my rabbi handing me a shovel to flick dirt into my
 father's grave
I think I see my father waving to me as he's lowered into the earth
I think I see my mother   blank-faced motionless her life changed
 after 43 years
I think I see my best friend wearing a suit and tie pointing mourners
 to open seats
I think I see my father standing and clapping at my high school
 graduation
I think I see my father poking a Sharpie at baseball players for
 autographs signed to me
I think I see my father reading *The Miami Herald* sports section
 sitting on a bus bench
I think I see childhood me figuring out how old I had to be until I
 became my father
I think I see childhood me counting minutes until my father came
 home from work

I'm not really seeing these things, am I?
I close my eyes and see the TV-blue flames
flicker fade to burnt gray ashes
but I don't really know
and these days I'm too old to truly see

Matzo Brei in Four Easy Steps

1. To create this Passover favorite, first take matzo, break into small pieces, place into a bowl. Cover with hot water for one minute. Squeeze out water.

Why is this night different from all other nights?
On all other nights we eat bread or matzo, while on this night we eat only matzo.

Too many nights we ate dinner with the TV on. I remember my father swearing the first time he saw Boy George on MTV.

Ashkenazi Jews are Jews of European descent. Ashkenazi Jews think they are better than other Jews.

2. In a small bowl, beat one egg with salt and pepper to taste and add to matzo. Mix well.

Why is this night different from all other nights?
On all other nights we eat all kinds of vegetables and herbs, but on this night we eat only bitter herbs.

My sister always defended Boy George. She used to dress up like him, same hats, braids, makeup, calling herself Girl Jill as she danced to the dinner table.

Sephardic Jews are Jews of middle-eastern and South American descent. Sephardic Jews think they are better than other Jews.

3. Heat frying pan with a little oil. Pour mixture into the pan.

Why is this night different from all other nights?
On all other nights we don't dip our vegetables in salt water, but on this night we dip them twice.

My mother picked dinner time to start fights with my father and my sister. Meals often ended with no one speaking to each other.

We called ourselves Jewish but we never really did any Jewish things except stay home from school on the Jewish Holidays and eat matzo brei on Passover. We thought we were better than other Jews.

4. Brown one side and turn over. Brown on the other.

Why is this night different from all other nights?
On all other nights we eat sitting upright, but on this night we eat reclining.

Boy George, known mostly as the gender-bending lead singer of Culture Club, a moderately successful mid-1980s pop group, is not Jewish.

My parents brought us up to think everyone was Jewish.
I once thought this true until my mother's complaints about the stores closing Christmas and Easter because of the *goyum*. She said the *goyum* thought they were better than Jews.

I grew up thinking we asked four questions on Passover. But it's really one question with four answers.

At George's Wake

Jonathan spoke openly about his father's death,
that he didn't have to worry about his dad's speechless
sort of pain anymore, the inaudible facial grimaces
doing all the complaining his voice refused to.
And Jonathan told me his mom would be fine in time,
she would stop crying herself to sleep every night,
she would one day be able to stand in her and his father's
bedroom, look in the wood-framed mirror above the bathroom vanity
and not see George standing behind her, his burly bear arms
enveloping her Victorian waist.

Yes, *mom would be fine,* Jonathan said, life would one day turn normal,
and on the nights he missed his father the most, he could look
to the skies and see one exploding star that would guide him
to where his father was in heaven. Or he could always put on an old
VCR tape of his dad clowning around in a Gators hat or Dolphins
t-shirt and it would be almost like having him back.

And he told me not to worry either. The weight now lifted,
none of us had to coordinate shuffles from doctor to doctor,
consult to consult, chemo visits where yesterday's hopes got swallowed
by today's despair, low blood counts or rampant fever out of nowhere.

Jonathan looked at my empty glass, placed on the kitchen table
between us, said I should get another one, and I got up,
kissed the top of his head,
stumbled out of the kitchen, past the mourners
whispering clichés in the living room,
slammed the bathroom door
and cried for Jonathan
now man of the house.

My Father's Armchair

I'd always feared turning into my father,
but when I saw the slacker teen standing on the corner,
and my head pinballed my father's familiar refrain:
"get a shave, get a haircut, get a job,"
I cupped my hands to my face, knowing
that if I designated a chair in my house as *'my chair,'*
the transition into my father would be complete.

My father's armchair was mauve, 1980s off-pink,
matching doilies on either arm rest, and he draped
a sky-blue blanket across the top. After work, he'd sit
in his chair in front of the TV until he fell asleep.
My father loved baseball, but especially the Dodgers,
and he loved lowbrow comedies, mostly *The Benny Hill Show*,
laughing a maniacal howl when he was watching.

When he fought his cancer, my father spent even more time
in his armchair. After he died, Mom asked me to drag it down
to their condo's garbage room where I noticed the bare,
worn-thin arm rests. At his sickest, he must have squeezed
them during the painful moments as the chemo failed,
holding tight to ride out relentless waves of agony.

When I got my father's armchair to the dumpster,
I set it up like he always did: same color doilies on the arm rests,
sky blue blanket across the top. Hoping to touch him a final time,
I felt a frayed armrest before walking away,
never once sitting in my father's armchair.

December 9, 1980

> *"Former Beatle John Lennon, the 40-year old*
> *lead singer of the most popular rock group in history,*
> *was shot to death last night outside his home."*
> -New York Daily News, 12/9/80

Engulfed by silence we sat.　　　　Dad's stoic blue mailman shirt
more wrinkled, he stared through vacant coffee stirs.
I spooned circles in my cereal bowl.　　　The news broke America.
Only Dad could tell me about John Lennon's murder
not Cosell, not Cronkite.　　We sat at the kitchen table
both as empty as the milk carton between us.　　I closed
my eyes and saw John　　　in white like he was crossing
Abbey Road　　　wave goodbye as he ascended.

Morning in Mourning

The sky cries, morning in mourning.
I don't know if the sun will rise today.
It's so fickle in its changing, sometimes
showing itself, sometimes hiding behind
whispered clouds, changing stories,
ashamed of the day.

The coffee maker speaks
to me in huffing and puffing,
the satellite TV fades in and out,
the toaster blows some bread
out its top, this milk smells sour.

When I was a kid, my father would order
me around the corner to see if it was raining.
Dying too soon, he left me on some gray street
corner to unravel all this on my own.

NYC Story, 1951-

1951:

On the day before my parents married,
the glowing couple stood outside a coffee shop in Union Square,
imagining two matching skyscrapers
would one day appear on that spot,
puncturing the sky with two holes that might lead
to another galaxy with another earth,
another postwar-proud USA and another New York,
where a reflecting about-to-be married couple
would look back at them, waving in technicolor unison.

1971:

Two towers stood majestic on that very spot
just as they envisioned. We watched the structures'
construction on TV every night from a Bronx
apartment in a far less grand building;
the same place my parents gathered neighbors
around their Formica console Zenith TV
gawking at the moonwalk two years earlier.

1972:

The last moon explorations ended in a yawn
and I learned when astronauts returned to Earth
they didn't slip through holes poked in the sky
by NYC towers, but splashed like a parachute
ballet into the California sea, strange
because they lifted off from a space center in Florida,
which is home to mostly New Yorkers now.

1975:

One night, Dad and I sat in the dark together
listening to a Mets game, counting stars
outside our window, telling me between innings
how he and Mom predicted those buildings perforating the sky
from lower Manhattan, and I didn't get it.

1994:

Someone tried to blow up the towers,
but they failed, the Towers stood, American strength
American power, American resilience.
Dad died that year during the baseball players' strike,
never knowing an assault on the Towers.

2001:

Someone tried to blow up the Towers,
and they did, American Airlines jets as weapons,
targeting American strength, American power,
American resilience, and American lives
innocent lives:
no parachutes for anyone to safely ballet land
the sky's holes empty and charred.

Mom cried watching this unfold on TV,
a different TV in a different apartment
but the same city, NYC, her city, America's city,
Dad's city, thankful he didn't see this.

2015:

I took my sons to a memorial dedicated
to the Towers and the lives lost when they fell.
I cried, my wife cried, my sons didn't get it.
Maybe next visit when the lunar-like craters
remaining are fully healed
and some about-to-be married couple
will stand in Union Square
imagining.

Mimeograph

Photograph   phonograph
      Spirograph   telegraph
I'm a father   I'm a son
      I've been called a mother
but I've never been one
      Gyroscope   stethoscope
give me love   give me hope
      earth circles around the sun
but doesn't rotate around anyone
      Colonoscope   kaleidoscope
give 'em enough rope
      paragraph   mimeograph
son an identical copy of his dad
      inheriting   what he had
      without the odorous ink
everything but the kitchen sink

Stuck Between Stations

After I'm dead, I'm sure my kids will curse me
for leaving the burden of sorting through my possessions,
scattered random papers, boxes and notebooks
shoved, pages bent, on shelves, ripped, yellowing.
Stacks of books in the closet, stealing space folded jeans
and sweaters should hold.

A man can accumulate a lot of worthlessness in his life.
I may as well sift through this now, revisit
my own history, place this stuff in its context, its time.

I find a spiral notebook and touch it like velvet,
twirling the ripped shreds embedded in those metal rings,
seeing my college girlfriend's swirling penmanship
on paper now thinner than my hair.

I can't let the kids think they're obligated to keep any of this.
I think of George Carlin's routine about how all his shit was stuff
and all my stuff was shit.

It's all shit to someone who didn't live the back story,
days chronicled upon days until they become lives
driving in circles, pushing buttons on car radios
drifting somewhere in the atmosphere
stuck between stations.

Ode to Derek Jeter

Derek Jeter can't be past 40—can he?
He can't have retired—can this be?

Where have you gone, Derek Jeter?
A nation turns its lonely eyes to you.

I'm sure it was yesterday or the day before or maybe last week
I saw him so young, in perfectly pressed polyester pinstripes,
pirouetting at shortstop as he threw a runner out at first.

It was only yesterday, right?
Say it ain't so, Joe.

I miss Jeter.
I miss hating him.
I miss hating him for being so damn perfect
yet wishing my own kids turned out like him.
I miss him because without him hating
the Yankees isn't as much fun.

I miss him because he reminds me of the days
my son would sit on my lap watching baseball
and we'd boo Jeter with every at bat.

I'm sure one day my son will miss watching sports with his son,
just like I miss watching sports with mine
just like my dad missed watching them with me,
all of us swatting away at the final outs as long as we can
even if it's just for a few more innings.

Incubation

My son drags his belongings on a squeaky dolly
into some state university dorm building universes
away balancing brown cardboard boxes, black
backpack, skateboard tucked
under his arm   he doesn't look back.

As he gets smaller with distance I see younger
me holding him the day he was born, whispering
attempts at wisdom to a face that seemed all eyes
as he inhaled his first of earth's labyrinth mysteries
under an incubation lamp   he could only look back.

Driving home something less than whole, I convince
myself this is the way it's supposed to be: he's an adult,
he's the future, and as Alligator Alley unrolls blacktop
and white lines, part of me is glad   he doesn't look back.

Macaroni & Cheese

My blue-eyed son   you rise
from the dinner table leaving dishes
lingering like nightfall. You have plans
to fulfill   schemes that exclude
your mom & me
but include nicknames   first names   fast
lanes   dates   vapes.

(As you run out the door
I see you in all your phases
like some whirling blur.
I see toddler you not eating
after the hurricane left us
no electricity
until I rigged up pans
on our backyard grill
boiling water   waiting for stubborn
noodles to unfold
knowing your favorite food
would make you happy & fill
your tummy.)

You rush off & after a time
I gather evening's pots & plates
scrape the cheese-plastered pan
with your teeth-printed spoon.

My blue-eyed son   you're a weed
blond & unbending
bridging shadows your 20th century
dad & 21st century hip-hop you

think we might see but we can never agree.

Twilight

The elderly man sitting at the table across from my son
and me, dressed in a powder blue sport coat
and white slacks, facing no one,
gazes once in a while at the red leather empty seat
in front of him, working over his fried rice and egg foo yung.
This is my son's favorite Chinese restaurant.
We've been coming here almost weekly his whole life.
It's getting darker outside; the old man's table is next to the window.
He's dining with his reflection.
I look at my son and then over at the man,
who slightly angles his head off to the side after each bite.
I wonder how quiet it must be to finish each day
alone, the person you thought you'd be with till death did you part
parting first.

**One Morning I Woke Up and There Was No One
to Take to Basketball Practice**

and the stairs creaked with each shallow step down
dampened winds blow through open windows whispering
voices and reverberating laughter off the walls of my boys' now empty
rooms. As the coffee maker puffs its conclusion, I lament
the times I complained about the bustling schedule,
the schlepping of kids from place to place, wishing
I could have those times back.
Perhaps one of the boys
will call me today
just to talk if
they aren't
too busy
living
their
lives.

Five Years

In five years, life will be so different, won't it be, honey?
The kids will be off to college,
and this house will
echo only with our talking
louder to one another
as our hearing fails
slowly. We'll turn into the Costanzas,
yelling even when we whisper.

And the stairs to the second-floor bedrooms?
You know the hundreds of times you wiped clean the sky-blue walls
from the black fingerprints, your scrubbing clear
the imprints where Adam, Jakob and Matt
used the wall instead of the bannister?
We could tell whose fingers the prints belonged
to by the height of the mark
and when the boys are gone,
I'm afraid you'll hold a rag out
looking to clean the stains
that aren't there, and you'll be lost,
wondering what to do next.

And when that happens,
we'll cry but we'll laugh, too,
together

then maybe send each of them a text saying "hi"
or even a "your parents miss you."
They won't think it's too corny,
they're good boys,
and maybe they'll miss us, too.

In five years we'll be marking the calendar
with black x's in broken crayon until the next long weekend,
the next semester break,
when we think they might come home
(if they don't have better plans)
and we'll make sure we have all their favorite
foods. You'll make empanadas;
I'll grill burgers and maybe we'll all share a beer
when they tell us they're now vegetarians.

But until then, this place will be really quiet.
And when the house gets hot in late afternoon,
I'll count the sun rays blinding me in the living room
as I read O'Hara or Ginsberg,
wishing you and me and the boys were young again.
I'll set the book in my lap and close my eyes
as I wait for you to come home,
so we can maybe whisk
the quiet to the woods out back
where it can calm the nerves
of the buzzing crickets
and we'll be able to hear ourselves
flirt again
like we did
when we were young.

Sunday Morning Poem

Sun rays like stripes cross through the blinds on the red wood floor, the coffee maker gurgles and puffs. I walk outside to get the *Post*. Bending over to pick up the paper gets harder each day. I breathe deep the weather, hold it in my lungs, go back inside.

The boys are still sleeping in their rooms; they're home this weekend. You sleep too, wrapped in blankets and hugging pillows, peaceful as outer space, and as far away. I like the warmth of this circle. I think I'll sit with the paper a bit and put a little extra sugar in my coffee.

David Colodney realized at an early age that he had no athletic ability whatsoever, so he turned his attention to writing about sports instead of trying to play them, covering everything from high school flag football to major league baseball for *The Tampa Tribune* and *The Miami Herald*. He grew up in a house where *The Miami Herald* sat awaiting him at the breakfast table, the *Miami News* was brought home by his father, and *USA Today* was his companion on the hourlong public bus rides he took to his Miami Beach home from school or work. Don't get this wrong, it's not like he read the whole thing cover-to-cover: all he cared about were the sports section and the features pages with record reviews, upcoming concert listings, and stories about the rock stars whose tours would bring them to now long-gone south Florida venues like the Hollywood Sportatorium and the Sunrise Musical Theatre.

David's father—who grew up in New York City and actually did read *The New York Times* and the *Daily News* cover to cover, daily—read a toddler David the paper like he read it to his illiterate mother, who couldn't read the papers for herself (as a refugee from Eastern Europe, she could only speak Yiddish, but could not read or write). The reading paid off in David's case: he learned to read at 4, and soon developed a love of writing, the sound of words, and how the words could have completely different meanings when placed in a different order in a sentence, or where a comma was placed, and so forth. David and his father had a paradoxical relationship in a way: close yet distant, but they never had any of the conflicts a lot of fathers and sons have. Instead, they drifted apart, like newspaper pages blowing down city streets, floating apart not only physically, but emotionally. David always said that his father never accepted the fact that he was growing up. Now that his own sons are on adulthood's brink, he knows he was right, but that's a natural feeling. It's ok to feel that way. David's also fascinated by the cyclical nature of the father-son relationship: a man may be a father, but he's also someone's son, being a copy of his father, spinning off copies in his sons, and like paper copies once spun through mimeograph machines, no two are exactly alike, but just similar enough "to do." It's in this space where these poems are born.

David holds an MFA from Converse College, and an MA from Nova Southeastern University. Mimeograph is his debut chapbook. His poetry has or will appear in a variety of journals including *St. Petersburg Review, South Carolina Review, Panoply,* and *The Chaffin Journal.* David serves as associate editor of *South Florida Poetry Journal* and lives in Boynton Beach, Florida with his wife, three sons, and golden retriever.

www.ingramcontent.com/pod-product-compliance
Lightning Source LLC
LaVergne TN
LVHW041312080426
835510LV00009B/966